FAILING

FORWARD

Turning Setbacks into Success

BRIAN LOCKRIDGE

L.P. Co.

Cover Illustration by: Gordon Johnson
Editors: Galen Lockridge & Daniel J. Tortora

ISBN: 979-8-9907039-0-2 (Paperback)
ISBN: 979-8-9907039-1-9 (Hardback)
ISBN: 979-8-9907039-2-6 (ebook)

First Edition: June 2024

Printed in the United States of America

Published by Lockridge Publishing Company (L.P. Co)
Mission Viejo, CA 92692
www.LockridgePublishingCompany.com

www.GirlDadUSA.com

To my wife, Galen, and our two daughters, Jordyn and London. You are what I prayed and longed for. I am a better man because of you.

I love you!

Contents

Discover Your Purpose

Have you ever experienced a longing for something better? Have you heard a compelling story that struck the inner core of your being? Are your fears driving you forward or derailing you down a path of regret? Are you feeling lost without a sense of purpose?

Life is not meant for us to live small. There is no joy in playing life safe and no reward for those not willing to lose. For what is potential without a dream? What is joy without sadness? Ultimately, what is success without failure?

In my life, I took many roads. Many were met with dead ends, and others were endless paths to nowhere. Looking back, the roads that took me the furthest were often the most difficult paths to take. Most seemingly began with no end in sight, but later revealed themselves as opportunities that continue to yield positive results. On life's journey, my successes quickly highlighted a picture, paralleled with acquiring responsibilities and overcoming adversity. With increased responsibility came an intrinsic desire to be better. Better not only for myself but also for those who put their trust in me.

My internal drive was a result of longing for a true sense of purpose in life. A purpose revealed through acquiring responsibility. In other words, I was required to step out of my comfort zone and make myself valuable to all those around me.

As we embark on our journey, we find ourselves navigating a maze of challenges and triumphs, seeking not only to guide others but to discover the depths of our very own character. It is difficult to know who we are, where we should go, and how we navigate life without knowing where we came from. We must first identify and face our past traumas, gather what we have learned from our experiences, and evaluate our key memories in order to move forward and take risks. *Failing Forward: Turning Setbacks into Success* is a compass, offering insights and wisdom to illuminate our own paths of self-discovery, leadership, and purpose.

1
Unveiling Your Identity

Close your eyes and take a deep breath…. Let your mind wander back to your earliest memories. Identify the moments that molded you into the person you are today. Recall the moments of joy, the challenges you faced, and the traumas you endured. Reflect on the significant moments of your childhood, adolescence, and adulthood. Consider the impact of your family dynamics, cultural background, and life experiences. Did you experience moments of joy and love, and were there periods of hardship and adversity? These are the moments that reveal who you are today. Accept and embrace them all, for they are the threads that form your identity.

Growing up in a family of six, I was the youngest of three boys. As I constantly tried to keep up with my older brothers, I reluctantly came to terms with my physical and mental limitations, realizing that I had started life at a disadvantage. Later, my world was upended when my parents divorced shortly after I turned 11 years old. Moving from place to place, I attended a total of six schools in a 5-year span. Due to the unexpected changes, my first move was difficult, but with each subsequent move, I became more adaptable. As the world I knew began to break apart, my mom accepted various jobs to provide for our family. One job, in particular, was when she started working as a janitor at the local elementary school. I recall spending countless hours in empty classrooms while she cleaned. My mom's job was demanding, both physically and mentally, but she performed it with unwavering dedication and pride. Her actions highlighted that there was dignity in all work and that every opportunity, no matter how small, was a chance to rise above circumstances. For this, I deeply admired my mother. Watching her scrub floors and clean classrooms late into the evening left an indelible mark on me. Her sacrifices taught me that hard choices were a part of life, and true strength lay in facing them head-on without shame.

As I grew older, I developed an affinity for sports while in high school, particularly the game of football. Along with friends, I joined the high school football team, where my initial performance was far from amazing. I was small, unsure, and often found myself at the bottom of the depth charts. Without prior experience, many, including myself, doubted that I would ever amount to much on the field, but I was determined to prove everyone wrong. Inspired by my mother's work ethic, I practiced tirelessly, staying late after team drills, studying plays, and conditioning my body.

Sophomore year marked a turning point in my football career. Despite being undersized compared to my teammates, I received an opportunity to play in a game. My heart raced as I ran onto the field, but my determination to succeed overshadowed my fears. With a toss play to the right, I dodged the first defender and ran the ball 76 yards to score my very first touchdown. Finally, my relentless practice paid off as I began to understand the nuances of the game. My courage, grit, and determination quickly caught the coach's attention, and soon I became a rising star on the team. What I lacked in size and experience, I made up for with perseverance.

While the world continued to change around me, my mom made another tough decision to let me move out of the house at the age of 15. Fortunately, I was blessed with the privilege of being taken in by three wonderful families: the Bosanko, Massaro, and Bahr families. Similar to my mom, these families also played a pivotal role in shaping who I am today.

By my junior year, my talent had continued to blossom, resulting in multiple scholarship offers due to my performance on the field. It was a reassuring moment that confirmed my beliefs in perseverance and hard work, especially for someone who had struggled and was unsure of his place on the field. One of the most fulfilling moments in my life was sharing this news with my mom, who had sacrificed so much for me.

Starting my collegiate football career, I was given the opportunity to start as a true freshman in our third game, against Florida State. The competition was fierce, and expectations were even higher, but I adapted quickly and became a contributing member of the team. Early on, injuries plagued me, testing my resolve as an athlete both on and off the field. Recalling the lessons learned from my mother's sacrifices and the adversities I overcame in high school, I refused to give up. I adjusted my training, focused on recovery, and fought my way back onto the field time and time again.

Each time I got knocked down, I rose stronger, embodying the resilience I had learned while growing up. Balancing my studies and football, I earned respect both as an athlete and a student. My journey became a testament to the power of hard work, humility, and perseverance. I realized that success was not about avoiding failure but about rising every time you fall.

After completing my football career and obtaining both a bachelor's and a master's degree, I began to apply the lessons I learned to my professional career. Since then, I have had the privilege of leading teams in various leadership roles within two Fortune 500 companies. My journey from a scared, small boy on the football field to a collegiate athlete was difficult, but it shaped me into a man who understood the true meaning of hard work and resilience.

Looking back at my life, I am blessed to be a younger brother, and even more so to have a mom who served as an example embodying strength and sacrifice. My mother's unspoken lessons as a janitor resonated deeply with me. I knew that no matter where life took me, I would carry her determination and humility with me.

Your past is not a burden to carry; in contrast, it is the badge that promoted you to who you are today. Each experience, whether positive or negative, has played a role in shaping who you are. Take a moment to acknowledge the strength and resilience you have shown in overcoming obstacles this far. Your story is uniquely yours, and it is worth exploring.

Peel back the layers of your identity like the pages of this book. Who are you when no one is watching? What are your deepest fears, desires, and dreams? Reflect on the roles you played in different aspects of your life as a child, sibling, friend, spouse, or colleague. Consider how these roles influenced your sense of self and your interactions with others. Explore your values, beliefs, and aspirations. What truly drives you? Allow yourself to be open, for in our vulnerabilities, we discover our strengths while addressing our weaknesses. Embrace the complexity of your life, for there is strength in every imperfection.

Past traumas may leave scars that run deep, but they do not define you without permission. Take the time to acknowledge the pain you have experienced and allow yourself to grieve and come to peace with your past. Seek support from loved ones or a therapist, if necessary. Healing is a journey that requires patience, reflection, and self-compassion as we navigate life.

Armed with a deep understanding of your past, begin to create a path forward with intention and purpose. Set goals that align with your values and aspirations. Cultivate meaningful relationships and pursue activities that bring you joy. Life is too short to live in the shadows of the past. Remember, you are the author of your story.

2

Life Experienced

In order to move forward, we must address our past. When faced with challenges, it is important to first identify the factors that restrict our ability to move forward. This chapter outlines four fundamental stages of resolution: *Catalyst, Reaction, Acceptance,* and *Resolution* (Figure 1). The four stages seek to reestablish a state of peace and highlight an intrinsic emotional response when navigating life, whether positive or negative.

When evaluating each stage, it is important to view the information through the lens of understanding that our perceptions shape our directions. A change in our perceptions can be the determining factor in changing how we behave and act within the world.

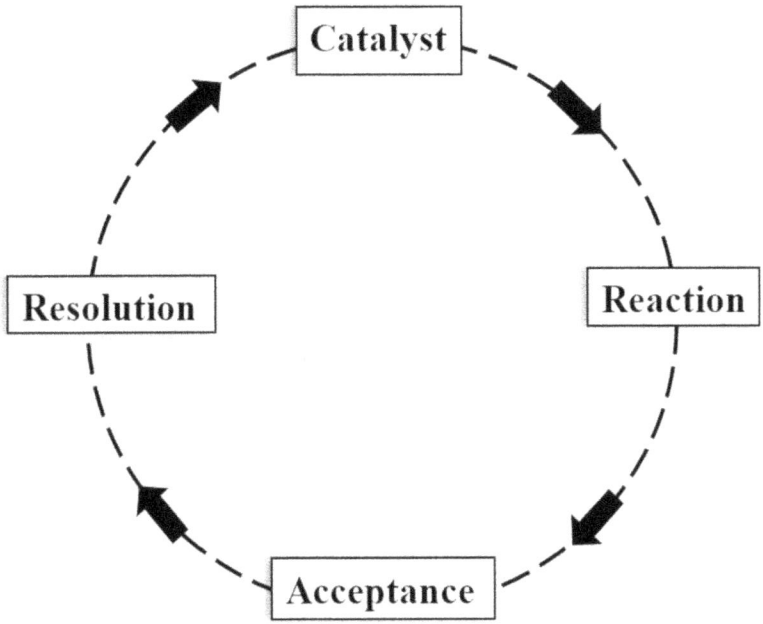

Figure 1. Four Stages of Resolution

Catalyst

A catalyst is a person or event that rapidly causes change or provokes us to act in a positive or negative manner. Embarrassment, failure, rejection, job loss, and other challenges all serve as catalysts that alter our behaviors in profound ways.

Embarrassment

Embarrassment is a particularly potent catalyst for behavioral changes, especially as an adolescent. Embarrassment occurs when we perceive that our actions fail to meet social norms or our own expectations, leading to feelings of shame or humiliation. This can happen in a variety of contexts, from making a mistake at work to stumbling over words in a social setting. Regardless of the specific circumstances, embarrassment can be a powerful motivator for change. It prompts us to reflect on our current behaviors and reconsider how we can avoid similar situations in the future. In some cases, embarrassment may result in a shift in our behavior as we distance ourselves from the sources of our humiliation.

We all experience embarrassment as a predictable outcome of attempting something new. At times, it leaves us feeling vulnerable and exposed in the process. As a result, embarrassment can negatively impact our self-esteem, further increasing our fears in social environments. If left to its devices, unresolved embarrassment can hinder how we perceive new challenges.

Failure

Whether it is a failed relationship, the loss of a job, or a setback in our personal goals, failure forces us to confront our limitations and compels us to reevaluate our approach to achieving our goals. Failure is a demotivating event that triggers feelings of inadequacy, disappointment, and self-doubt. As a result, we may engage in negative self-talk, replaying the event over and over in our heads, or calling into question our capabilities in both the present and in the future. Constant failure can condition us to avoid taking risks or pursuing new opportunities altogether.

While failure can be demoralizing, it can also serve as a valuable learning tool. Failure presents an opportunity for resilience, perseverance, and the importance of adaptability. Many successful people attribute their achievements to the lessons they learned through past failures. This demonstrates that failure can ultimately lead to growth and success.

Major Life Events

In most cases, major life events cause us to reassess our beliefs, our behaviors, and our priorities in life. Whether it is a major accident or our parents' divorce, our negative experiences embed rooted trauma that can evoke intense emotional responses such as grief, fear, resentment, and shame. The way we respond to these catalysts can vary, but they often result in a period of introspection, growth, and ultimately, transformation, either negatively or positively.

One major life event that can significantly alter how we behave is the experience of death, particularly the loss of a loved one. Although death is an inevitable part of life, it often disrupts our physical and mental being, leaving a ripple effect that alters our perspectives of the world around us. When someone close to us passes, it triggers a range of emotions such as grief, sadness, anger, and even guilt.

The loss of a loved one can lead to a period of intense grieving, which we may struggle to completely come to terms with. The loss can manifest in various ways, including withdrawal from social activities, developing poor coping techniques, loss of concentration, changes in appetite or sleep patterns, and an overall sense of numbness.

Furthermore, the passing of a loved one may prompt us to reevaluate our relationships, priorities, and goals, leading to profound shifts in perspective and behavior. We may become inspired to live life to the fullest or cherish the moments we have with our loved ones still present. Others may associate a recent passing with the fear of future losses and find it difficult to overcome the uncertainties of life. This fear can lead to mental paralysis, preventing us from fully engaging with life.

The loss of a loved one is challenging, but it is also an encouraging catalyst for growth, resilience, and a deepening of our understanding of what it means to be human. Through the process of mourning and reflection, we learn how to navigate the complexities of loss and emerge stronger, more compassionate, and feeling more willing to take control of our lives.

Accidents

Accidents or near-death experiences may also be catalysts that alter our behaviors. Whether minor or severe, accidents can have far-reaching consequences for us all. In addition to physical injuries, accidents can also cause emotional trauma and psychological distress.

Following an accident, we may experience a range of emotions including fear, anger, and anxiety. We may struggle with feelings of guilt or self-blame, especially if we believe the accident could have been avoided. In some cases, the fear of experiencing another accident can result in avoidance behaviors or heightened vigilance in certain situations. Accidents can compel us to apply increased countermeasures within our own lives as well as to those around us. Although prevention is the means, this approach can also negatively impact our social circles as well as other areas of our lives.

Family Relationships

Family relationships can also be a significant catalyst for behavioral changes. Dysfunction within the family unit, such as lack of family connection, loss of trust, family pressures, or divorce, can all have lasting effects on our emotional well-being and behaviors. Growing up in an unstable family environment can shape how we view ourselves in relation to others. This may lead to difficulties in forming healthy, long-term relationships and navigating social situations.

Economic upbringing can also have similar effects on how we behave. Children who are raised in poverty, neglect, or violent environments can develop maladaptive coping mechanisms and struggle to regulate their emotions. They may also have difficulties trusting others or forming secure attachments, which can impact relationships as well as implicate how they assimilate within society.

Regardless of the catalyst, these experiences can be painful and difficult to navigate, but they also offer opportunities for growth, resilience, and transformation. By confronting our past head-on and embracing the lessons offered, we will emerge stronger, wiser, and more aware of the influences that shape our behaviors today.

Reflection Questions

➤ Reflecting back on your life, list three life-altering catalysts you experienced?

➤ What was the catalyst that impacted you the most?

➤ How old were you during this event?

➤ How often do you think about this event?

➤ Does this event shape who you are today? If yes, how so?

Reaction

A reaction is a physiological or psychological response experienced as a result of a situation or event (catalyst). Our initial reactions when faced with a challenge, grief, or fear are complex yet visible to all those around us. Reactions can be influenced by a variety of factors such as personality, past experiences, and coping mechanisms. Understanding our initial reactions can shed light on the ways we navigate difficult situations.

Common Reactions to Challenges

Shock and Denial: This can manifest itself as an initial disbelief as to the magnitude of the challenge. Shock or denial reveals that the mind may need time to process the information and come to terms with the new reality.

Fight or Flight Response: When confronted with challenges, the instinctive "fight or flight" response is often activated. Some of us may lean towards the "fight" response. This physiological reaction prepares us to confront the threat or flee from it. The immediate instinct to protect yourself is a natural response to perceived dangers. We may approach challenges with a proactive and assertive attitude, ready to tackle the issue head-on. This could also manifest as a drive to overcome obstacles, to take charge and find solutions, or even to take foolish risks.

Increased Alertness: We may become hyper-vigilant agents, scanning our environment for signs of danger. This heightened awareness is an adaptive response to enhance our survival, as in self-preservation.

We may feel compelled to project strength and confidence to conceal any feelings of fear in the process. This projection is often a defense mechanism when our capabilities are questioned due to our vulnerabilities.

Stress and Anxiety: Challenges often evoke stress and anxiety. The uncertainty and pressures associated with a challenge can trigger the body's stress responses, leading to heightened emotions, racing thoughts, and physical tension. This physiological response is a natural reaction to the threats we perceive. Emotions may surge rapidly and unpredictably, making it challenging for us to navigate our feelings in the initial stages of grief.

Emotional Suppression: In some cases, we might downplay our emotional reactions and begin to focus on practical solutions, rather than expressing vulnerability. This can be a coping mechanism to avoid being perceived as weak or not in control of our emotions.

Delayed Emotional Expression: Many might experience a delay in expressing grief openly. This delay could be due to the need to process emotions internally before feeling comfortable sharing them with others.

Isolation or Seeking Support: We may initially prefer to deal with challenges in isolation, attempting to handle issues on our own. The overwhelming emotions may prompt a desire for introspection and processing the loss privately before engaging with a broader support system. On the other hand, we may recognize the importance of seeking support from friends, family, or professional networks.

Avoidance Behavior: Fear can lead to avoidance behavior, where we actively try to evade the source of fear. The avoidance may provide a temporary sense of relief but can also reinforce the fear over time.

Coping Mechanisms: We often resort to various coping mechanisms in the initial stages of grief. This can include engaging in activities (positive or negative) that bring comfort and attempting to seek solace in routines. This approach to coping may serve as a distraction and a way to channel emotions into something productive.

Physical Symptoms: Grief can manifest not only emotionally but physically as well. In instances of grief, we may experience symptoms such as fatigue, changes in appetite, or difficulty sleeping during the initial phase of grief.

<u>Reflection Questions</u>

> ➢ When faced with challenges, how do you typically respond?

> ➢ How long does your response to an event last?

> ➢ Does your initial response yield the results you expect?

> ➢ What approach do you take when addressing challenges?

> ➢ Do challenges deter you or motivate you? Why?

Acceptance

The acceptance phase is a critical juncture in our emotional and psychological journeys as individuals. The acceptance phase involves coming to terms with the reality of the situation, acknowledging the emotions associated with it, and finding a way forward. Of all phases, acceptance is the most pivotal when overcoming adversity. Without acceptance, a resolution cannot truly be identified, further diminishing our ability to properly close chapters and peacefully move forward. Let's explore how people commonly react or behave during the acceptance phase in each of these scenarios.

Acknowledgment and Realism: In the acceptance phase, we move beyond denial and acknowledge the reality of our circumstances. Shifting towards a more realistic appraisal of the situation, we begin to recognize the ongoing challenges and limitations involved. The intense emotions felt in the initial stages may give way to a more stable emotional state, allowing us to approach the situation with a clearer mindset.

Adaptation and Flexibility: Acceptance often involves adapting to new circumstances and demonstrating flexibility in how we navigate the experience. We may reassess our goals and expectations, modifying them to align with the changed reality. This adaptability is crucial for navigating challenges effectively.

Problem-Solving and Planning: With acceptance comes a renewed focus on problem-solving. In this phase, we may spend time focusing on analyzing the challenge, breaking down the issue into manageable parts, and formulating strategies to overcome it. This proactive approach mostly stems from a willingness to take control of the situation while utilizing the constraints presented. We immediately shift into a problem-solving mode. This proactive approach is often driven by a desire to regain a sense of control in order to return to a state of normalcy.

Seeking Support and Resources: Acceptance does not necessarily mean facing challenges alone. We may actively seek support from others, whether through collaboration with peers or mentors or by leveraging available resources. Within the acceptance phase, the willingness to ask for help is easier due to our ability to see the situation for what it truly is.

Integration of Loss: Acceptance in the context of grief involves integrating the reality of the loss into our lives. This does not mean forgetting or minimizing the significance of the loss, but rather finding a way to coexist with it. We may gradually assimilate the loss into our identity.

Creating Meaning: Acceptance provides an opportunity for us to create meaning. This could involve seeking a higher sense of purpose, identifying lessons learned, or honoring the memory of what or who was lost. In creating meaning, we contribute to the healing process.

Rebuilding Identity: Grief can reshape our identity, but acceptance allows us to redefine who we are. As we progress, we begin to explore new aspects of ourselves, redefine our current roles, and develop resilience in the face of adversity. The acceptance phase is marked by a willingness to embrace a transformed identity.

Gradual Return to Routine: Acceptance involves a gradual return to routine and normalcy. While the pain of loss may persist, we start to engage in daily activities and commitments, recognizing that life continues even in the aftermath of grief.

Normalization of Fear Responses: In the acceptance phase of fear, we begin to normalize fear as a natural yet adaptive response. There is an acknowledgment that fear is a part of the human experience and that we can coexist with it through courage and resilience.

Exposure and Desensitization: Acceptance involves a willingness to confront fear through exposure. We may deliberately expose ourselves to the source of fear gradually, leading to the desensitization or dissolution of our fears. This process helps us reduce the intensity of our fears over time.

Self-Compassion: Acceptance of fear often involves cultivating self-compassion. We may recognize that experiencing our fears does not make us weak or inadequate. Instead, we embrace grace as a way to navigate fear with forgiveness and understanding that we may or may not always be successful in our attempts.

In summary, the acceptance phase is characterized by a profound shift in mindset and behavior. It marks the transition from initial shock and resistance to a more constructive engagement with the challenge, grief, or fear. The acceptance phase is not about erasing the past or minimizing the challenges faced. It is about finding a way to coexist, adapt, and move forward with resilience and understanding. It is a dynamic and transformative process that contributes significantly to our growth and well-being.

<u>Reflection Questions</u>

➢ What is one major challenge or life event that impacted your life?

➢ Have you truly accepted the reality of this life-changing event?

➢ If not, why? What is holding you back?

➢ Are you willing to let go? If not, why?

➢ Is not being able to accept the reality of what happened getting in the way of progressing or living a fulfilled life?

Resolution

The resolution phase of overcoming challenges, grief, and fear is a critical stage where we, who fully accept the reality of our catalyst, begin to implement strategies to move forward and regain a sense of peace. Here is a detailed analysis of how we commonly behave in the resolution phases.

Sense of Accomplishment: Successfully overcoming a challenge often brings a sense of accomplishment or relief. We may experience a boost in energy, confidence, or self-esteem as we recognize our ability to tackle tough challenges. With a new outlook, we accept our ability to face future challenges. As we rebuild, we may celebrate our achievements independently or with those close to us.

Reflection and Learning: The resolution phase provides an opportunity to reflect on the journey from the beginning to the end. We may analyze the strategies that were implemented, identify areas for improvement, and extract valuable lessons learned from the experience. This reflective process contributes to our personal growth and to the further development of resolutions for future use.

Integration of New Skills: Successfully navigating a challenge often involves acquiring new skills or honing existing skills. In the resolution phase, we may actively integrate our newfound skills into our lives while fostering a sense of empowerment and adaptability.

Setting New Goals: Having overcome a challenge, we may be inspired to set new goals within our lives. The resolution phase can become a platform for envisioning the future and channeling our abilities into pursuing new endeavors.

Reinvestment in Life: As grief resolves, we may reinvest our energy and emotions in other aspects of life. This could include pursuing passions, engaging in activities that bring joy, and reestablishing a sense of purpose.

Supporting Others: Having experienced grief, we may become a source of support for others facing similar challenges. The resolution phase may inspire a desire to help others navigate their grief journeys, creating a sense of community and empathy. This altruistic behavior can serve as a positive outcome of the resolution phase, turning personal pain into a source of strength for others.

Building Resilience: Successfully confronting and overcoming fear contributes to our increased resilience to life around us. We may find that we are better equipped to face future fears with a more adaptive mindset and a strengthened sense of self.

Learning and Growth: The resolution phase of fear is often accompanied by a commitment to ongoing learning, growth, and willingness to take more risks. We may seek to understand the root causes of our fears, addressing them through personal development, education, or acquiring new skills.

Therapeutic Interventions: Seeking professional help, such as therapy or counseling, is a common approach during the resolution of fear. Therapeutic interventions may provide us with tools to manage and overcome persistent fears, fostering emotional well-being.

Embracing Change: Conquering fear often involves embracing change. The resolution phase demonstrates our willingness to adapt, try new experiences, and step outside our comfort zones as we move forward.

The resolution phase is a critical stage where we navigate the aftermath and actively work towards healing and growth. While there are common themes, each person's journey is uniquely shaped by personal experiences and coping mechanisms. Encouraging self-reflection, seeking support when needed, and embracing the lessons learned are key elements that contribute to our successful resolution of overcoming future challenges, grief, or fears. The four stages seek to manage a world between chaos and peace. The ultimate goal of the four stages is to return to our natural state of being, which is peace. Reunited with peace, we are now able to step forward in life with confidence and a clear mind.

Reflection Questions

➢ After accepting the events that impacted you, what steps are you willing to take to initiate the resolution phase?

➢ Identify the steps you are not "willing" to take. Why?

➢ Looking within, what is truly preventing you from taking the next step? What fears or feelings are you experiencing?

➢ Developing a plan to overcome your inner conflicts. How can you safely implement goals and objectives to challenge yourself to take the next step?

➢ When will you implement and/or initiate your next steps?

3

Life Hack:
The Three A's

How to accelerate the resolution of challenges, grief, and fear?

Instead of investing time in accepting and resolving challenges, we tend to spend more time on the direct and indirect emotional outcomes of an occurrence. This chapter uncovers a way to expedite resolutions to challenges, grief, and fears encountered in our everyday lives. These techniques will provide stability in moments where life, as you know it, may seem uncertain.

When facing challenges, utilize the "Three A's" (figure 2) to effectively manage and accelerate resolution. In order of operation, the Three A's are *Accept*, *Assess*, and *Adjust*.

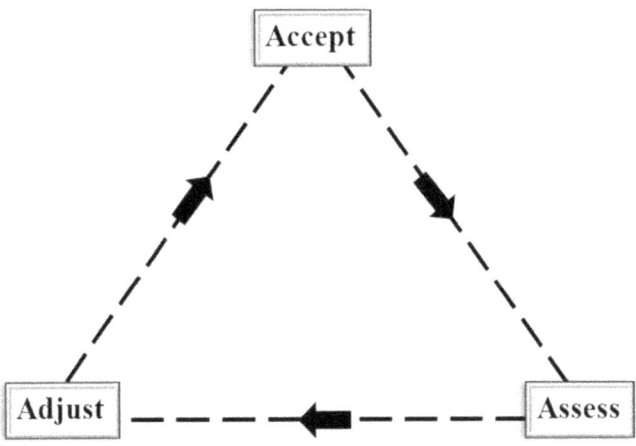

Figure 2. The Three A's of Life

Accept

Acceptance is the first step towards overcoming a challenging situation. This approach involves acknowledging the reality of the circumstances, including any emotions that arise from them, without denying or suppressing them. Acceptance does not mean giving up or resigning yourself to fate; rather, it is about recognizing that the situation exists and that we must face it.

As a running back, my journey within the game of football was a constant battle filled with fear. Playing that position, I had to face the inevitability of taking on larger opponents, pound-for-pound, while absorbing hits play after play. With each collision, I risked being sprawled on the field, seriously hurt, or gasping for air. Pain was the physical reality of the sport—a sport that was relentless and punishing, with the inescapable reality of getting hurt.

My ability to rise and face another play stemmed from accepting the terms of the game and embracing them as my own. It marked a turning point when I realized that success on the field extended beyond mere speed or strength. Over time, the once-feared bruises and scars accumulated into symbols of my resilience and unwavering dedication to confront my fears with every play.

In terms of grief, acceptance is crucial, as our emotions can be overwhelming and difficult to process. By accepting the reality of our loss, we are able to begin the process of moving towards a resolution as we take steps towards healing and growth.

Someone who has lost a loved one may initially struggle to accept the loss and may experience denial or disbelief. However, by gradually coming to terms with the loss we allow ourselves to grieve and begin the process of healing. Through acceptance we find meaning in our experience and ultimately conclude with a sense of peace as we move forward.

When addressing fears, psychologists use exposure therapy as a specific form of cognitive behavioral therapy while treating patients. Exposure therapy involves systematically confronting the feared stimulus or situation to reduce fear and avoidance behaviors. According to psychologists, this approach is based on the principle of habituation, which suggests that repeated exposure to the feared stimulus can lead to decreased anxiety over time. Fundamentally, exposure seeks to first accept the fear at hand. It then addresses what needs to be done to mitigate the fear with each occurrence.

Assess

Once accepted, the next step is to assess the situation or emotions associated with the problem. This involves examining the underlying factors that contributed to the change and analyzing the feelings and behaviors that arise from it.

Assessing the cause or emotions of an event requires introspection and self-awareness. It may involve asking yourself questions such as "How do I feel?" or "Why do I feel the way I do?" This process can help us gain clarity and insight into our experiences, allowing us to better understand our own thoughts, feelings, and behaviors.

While I accepted the terms of the game of football, I needed to assess the fears I associated with the game. In my case, it was simply the fear of being hurt and not being a contributing member of the team.

Like many, fear is a powerful driver that influences our actions. It can be both rational and irrational, varying widely depending on individual experiences and contexts. Fear encompasses everything from immediate, tangible threats to more abstract concerns about the future, social acceptance, or personal failure. Although fear is an intrinsic feeling, it often originates externally and permeates into our daily lives.

As a survival mechanism, fear alerts us to potential dangers and guides our responses. However, fear also profoundly shapes our perceptions and behaviors, often impacting our decisions more than we realize. To understand where we place our fears, we must explore how fear manifests in our lives, its sources, and its effects on our daily existence.

While assessing my fears, I discovered that we all encounter two forms of fear: (1) fear that hinders progress and (2) fear that propels us forward. Where we position our fears determines our behavior within the world. Serving as a barrier, placing our fears in front of us often obstructs our forward movement. In contrast, when we place our fears behind us, we use fear as a driving force for change and progress. In essence, fear can either enable us to act or prevent us from doing so.

Adjust

After accepting and assessing, the final step is to adjust to the situation and adapt accordingly. Adjustment involves applying the necessary changes to our behavior and mindset to cope with the challenges at hand. Adjusting to the situation requires resilience, flexibility, and a willingness to learn. It may involve acquiring new skills, seeking support, or making changes to our environment. This process can be gradual and may require patience and perseverance.

For example, someone who has lost their job may need to adjust to the new reality of unemployment. Spending time updating their resume, networking, and exploring new career opportunities is a form of adjusting to life as they know it. Similarly, someone who has experienced a significant loss may need to adjust to life without their loved one by finding new sources of support and meaning, while expanding on the lessons learned from those no longer with us.

In terms of football, I decided to accept the terms of the game, placed my fears behind me, and worked harder to prepare mentally and physically for every opponent. In doing so, I was able to overcome my fears both on and off the field.

When overcoming our challenges, grief, or fears, we should incorporate the Three A's into our decision-making process. By accepting the reality of the situation, assessing the cause of our emotions, and adjusting accordingly, we are more equipped to develop strategies during challenging times. While this process may be challenging, the Three A's can accelerate resolution of challenges we faced and ultimately lead to personal growth, healing, peace, and a renewed sense of strength.

4
Life Hack:
Optimism

How to accelerate the resolution of challenges, grief, and fear?

"A successful person begins with two beliefs: the future can be better than the present, and I have the power to make it so."—David Brooks

Often overlooked, optimism has profound effects on various aspects of our lives. Optimism is a powerful mindset characterized by a positive outlook on life, a belief in our ability to overcome challenges, and a hopeful attitude towards the future. This chapter explores how optimism positively effects mental health, physical well-being, relationships, and overall quality of life.

Psychological Well-Being

Research has shown that optimistic individuals tend to experience lower levels of anxiety, depression, and stress compared to those who are more pessimistic.

With an estimated 40 million adults impacted each year, anxiety disorders are the most prevalent class of mental illness within the United States (US Burden of Disease Collaborators, 2013). Studies have linked an increase in optimism via orbitofrontal cortex (OFC) gray matter volume to the reduction of anxiety. "Trait optimism mediated the relation between the left OFC volume and anxiety, thus demonstrating that increased gray matter volume in this brain region protects against symptoms of anxiety through increased optimism" (Dolcos S., Hu Y., Iordan A. D., Moore M., Dolcos, F., 2016).

Due to the malleability of the brain, our thoughts can shape how we interact with the world around us. Optimism is a bio-psychological marker of resilience against emotional dysregulation, especially in terms of anxiety symptoms. In other words, optimism serves as protective armor against mental health disorders by promoting resilience and coping mechanisms for negative thinking.

Individuals with optimistic traits tend to have better coping skills and a more adaptive response to adversity, allowing them to bounce back quickly from setbacks while maintaining a sense of hope and resilience in challenging times. Optimistic individuals have significantly lower levels of depression, which can affect the way we behave and interact with others. Optimistic individuals are more likely to engage in positive self-talk, which contributes to our ability to quickly overcome difficult situations. Optimism is also linked to higher levels of self-esteem, self-efficacy, and a larger sense of meaning.

Optimistic individuals tend to approach challenges with a "can-do" attitude and have a belief in their ability to find creative solutions. This mindset fosters a growth-oriented mentality that encourages continuous learning and personal development. Optimism also improves decision-making skills, as individuals are more likely to focus on opportunities rather than dwell on potential obstacles or failures.

Physical Health

The benefits of optimism extend well beyond mental health as well. Studies have found that optimistic individuals have a lower risk of developing chronic diseases such as heart disease, hypertension, diabetes, and stroke. Optimistic individuals tend to engage in healthier behaviors such as regular exercise, balanced nutrition, and adequate sleep, which contribute to overall well-being and longevity. In addition, optimism has been shown to boost the immune system and enhance resilience in the face of illness or injury.

Relationships

Optimism plays a crucial role in fostering healthy and fulfilling relationships. Optimistic individuals are more likely to approach interpersonal conflicts with a positive outlook, seeking solutions and compromise rather than harboring resentment or blame. Optimism also enhances communication skills, empathy, and emotional intelligence, which are essential for building and maintaining strong connections with others. In romantic relationships, optimism can promote intimacy, trust, and mutual support, leading to greater relationship satisfaction and longevity.

Ultimately, optimism contributes to a higher quality of life by shaping one's perception of the world and future possibilities. Optimistic individuals tend to experience greater life satisfaction, fulfillment, and happiness, even in the face of adversity. They approach life with a sense of purpose and meaning, viewing challenges as opportunities for growth and learning rather than obstacles. Optimism fosters a sense of hope and resilience that empowers us to overcome setbacks and pursue our goals with confidence and determination. By embracing optimism, we can lead happier, healthier, and more fulfilling lives.

5
Life Hack:
Competition

How to accelerate the resolution of challenges, grief, and fear?

Success is not determined by wins or losses. True success is measured by one's ability to overcome adversity through determination and adaptability.

Competition is a fundamental aspect of human nature, driving us to push ourselves beyond our limits and strive for excellence. While some view competition in a negative light, citing concerns over increased stress, comparison, and rivalry, it also holds the potential for positive impacts on personal growth and improvement. In this chapter, we will explore the case for embracing competition as a catalyst for self-improvement while exploring the positive effects it can have on those of us who seek to better ourselves.

Motivation and Goal Setting

Competition can provide us with a clear benchmark for measuring our progress and performance in relation to others. By setting goals and striving to outperform our competitors, we become motivated to work harder, stay focused, and continuously improve. Competition encourages us to push beyond our comfort zones and reach for higher levels of achievement, leading to increased self-confidence and a sense of accomplishment.

Innovation and Creativity

As we seek to differentiate ourselves, competition fosters innovation and creativity to gain a competitive edge. The pressure to "outdo" our competition often sparks new ideas, solutions, and approaches to solving problems. Competition encourages us to think outside the box, experiment with new strategies, and embrace failure as a steppingstone to success. Through competition, we are challenged to adapt, evolve, and innovate, driving progress and advancement in various fields and industries.

Resilience and Adaptability

Competing in a challenging and dynamic environment builds resilience and adaptability, which is essential for navigating the uncertainties of life. The experience of facing setbacks, failures, and obstacles in competition teaches us valuable lessons in perseverance, grit, and determination. By learning to bounce back from defeat and adapt to changing circumstances, we develop the resilience needed to overcome adversity and thrive in the face of challenges.

Collaboration and Teamwork

While competition is often portrayed as a solo endeavor, it also fosters collaboration and teamwork as we come together to achieve common goals. Competing alongside others encourages us to leverage our strengths, support one another, and work towards a shared vision of success. Through collaboration, we learn the importance of communication, trust, and mutual respect, skills that are essential for success both in competition and in life.

Personal Growth and Self-Discovery

Ultimately, competition serves as a catalyst for personal growth and self-discovery, allowing us to uncover our strengths, weaknesses, and potential. Competition challenges us to confront our limitations, confront our fears, and push beyond our perceived boundaries. Through competition, we discover what we are truly capable of, unlocking our full potential and realizing our dreams.

While competition is often feared or misunderstood, it holds the power to drive us to greater heights of achievement and fulfillment. By embracing competition as a tool for personal growth and improvement, we can harness its positive impacts to become the best versions of ourselves. Whether in sports, academics, or the workplace, competition serves as a powerful force for driving progress, innovation, and excellence in all aspects of life.

6
Life Hack:
Impacts of Gratitude

How to accelerate the resolution of challenges, grief, and fear?

Gratitude is a powerful emotion that can transform how we view the world. When we cultivate a mindset of gratitude, we shift our focus from what we lack to what we have. This frame of thinking leads to a greater sense of happiness, resilience, and overwhelming joy in life. In this chapter, we will explore the impacts of being grateful and how practicing gratitude can enhance various aspects of our lives.

Enhanced Mental Health

One of the most significant impacts of being grateful is on our mental health. When we express gratitude, our brains release neurotransmitters such as dopamine and serotonin, which are known to improve mood and

promote feelings of happiness and contentment. By acknowledging and appreciating the positive aspects of our lives, we can cultivate a more optimistic outlook and build emotional resilience in the face of challenges.

Improved Physical Health

In addition to its effects on mental health, gratitude has also been linked to improved physical health outcomes. Studies have found that individuals who regularly practice gratitude experience benefits such as lower blood pressure, better immune function, and reduced inflammation. Grateful individuals are also more likely to engage in health-promoting behaviors such as exercise, healthy eating, and regular medical checkups. By fostering a sense of appreciation for our bodies and our overall well-being, gratitude can contribute to better health outcomes and overall longevity.

Strengthened Relationships

Gratitude plays a vital role in nurturing and strengthening our relationships with others. When we express gratitude towards those around us, whether friends, family, or colleagues, we deepen our connections and foster a sense of mutual respect and appreciation. As grateful individuals, we are more likely to be empathetic, compassionate, and supportive in our interactions with others, leading to greater trust and intimacy in our relationships. By cultivating an ethos of gratitude in our personal and professional lives, we can create more fulfilling and meaningful connections with those around us.

Increased Resilience

In times of adversity or hardship, gratitude can serve as a powerful tool for building resilience. By reframing challenges as opportunities for growth and learning, grateful individuals are better equipped to bounce back from setbacks and persevere in the face of adversity. Gratitude helps us find meaning and purpose even in difficult circumstances, allowing us to navigate life's ups and downs with greater resilience and strength.

Practical Tips for Cultivating Gratitude

Incorporating gratitude into our daily lives doesn't have to be complicated. Simple practices such as keeping a gratitude journal, expressing appreciation to others, and taking time to savor life's little pleasures can have a profound impact on our overall well-being. By making gratitude a habit, we can reap its many benefits and transform our lives in meaningful and lasting ways.

7

Life Hack:
Discovering Purpose

How to accelerate the resolution of challenges, grief, and fear?

Whether you believe in God or not, we are all created with a purpose. This is why we intrinsically long for a sense of meaning for why we exist. In other words, we find ourselves asking, "What is our purpose in life?" or "Why are we always searching for a sense of fulfillment?" **It becomes clear that in the absence of purpose, life is a void without direction—simply chaos.** While often compared to animals, humans are uniquely different in that we all understand and foresee our inevitable future—a future that can be joyful, but also rattled with pain, suffering, brokenness, and ultimately death. So why live? What is the purpose? In other words, we are asking, "What is the meaning of our lives?"

Understanding that life can be filled with pain and suffering, we begin to live life with aspirations of mitigating the hurt and suffering along the way. We create guidelines and social behavioral norms to reduce conflict and keep the peace. We understand, consciously or not, that our actions do affect the world around us and are a reflection on our outcomes. Still, we manage to seek a sense of purpose in life as we know it. One powerful motivator for uncovering purpose is through acquiring responsibility in our daily lives. Responsibility evokes commitment, sacrifice, and the necessity to serve others. Through responsibility, in a chaotic world, we create the "why" in order to face the "how." At its root, responsibility provides us with something to chase, gain, and fight for. In return, our responsibilities enforce the need to improve and better ourselves.

Life can be conceptualized into a single thought process that states, "I am currently here, and I need to be there." 'Here' refers to the state in which you find your current self as you are today. 'There' refers to the state in which you hope your current self will soon be tomorrow. In a sense, you are always working towards or managing the state in between the 'here' and the 'there.' Jordan Peterson states in his book *Maps of Meaning: The Architecture of Belief* (1999), "We posit a goal, in image and word, and we compare present conditions to that goal. We evaluate the significance of ongoing events in light of their perceived relationship to the goal. We modify our behavioral outputs – our means – when necessary, to make the attainment of our goal ever more likely. We modify our actions within the game but accept the rules without question. We move in a linear direction from present to future" (pgs. 34–35).

In other words, we are constantly engaged in a life that attempts to bridge the gap between "What is?" and "What should be?" As we progress through life, we intrinsically grapple with the relationship between what the undesirable present is and what the desirable future should be. In doing so, we are constantly questioning "how we should act" in a given moment in order to get to where we desire to be. The question of how we should act should be centered on arranging a planned sequence of behaviors that position us for a successful outcome, close to or beyond our desired outcomes. We must accept our ability to shape the future and be willing to forego life's pleasures while adopting responsibility as a means to success.

Sacrifice often goes hand in hand with pursuing our purpose, as it requires us to make difficult choices. Sacrifice can come in many forms, whether it's time, money, comfort, or personal desires. By embracing sacrifice as a necessary part of growth and development, individuals can unlock new opportunities for self-discovery and transformation on their journey towards purpose.

At times, necessity drives us to discover our purpose out of sheer survival or need. When faced with challenges, adversity, or life circumstances, individuals may be compelled to step up, adapt, and find creative solutions to overcome obstacles. Necessity can spark innovation, resilience, and a sense of purpose as we rise to meet the demands of the moment and navigate through uncertainty.

Discovering your purpose through responsibility, commitment, sacrifice, and necessity is a journey that requires courage, resilience, and self-awareness. By embracing these elements and taking intentional action towards what truly matters to you, you can uncover a sense of purpose and fulfillment that drives you forward on your path to living a meaningful and purposeful life.

8
Failing Forward

"Our greatest weakness lies in giving up. The most certain way to succeed is always to try just one more time." — Thomas Edison

In January 1879, in Menlo Park, New Jersey, Thomas Edison invented the light bulb, creating a high-resistance, incandescent electric light. Among the many inventions created by Edison, the light bulb changed how we experienced the night forever. Prior to his passing, Edison patented 1,093 of his inventions, including the telephone receiver, microphone, storage batteries, and the electric pen. Although Edison is known today for his inventions, his greatest contribution to the world was his persistence in the face of failure. He stated, "I have not failed 10,000 times. I've successfully found 10,000 ways that will not work... I was never myself discouraged or

46

inclined to be hopeless of success. I cannot say the same for all my associates."

Intrinsic to us all is the ability to develop a belief that success is not void of failure; rather, success can only be derived from failure itself. Similar to practicing, success stems from a series of repetitive events that reshape and reform us through the constant improvement from one failure to another. It is important to understand that success is not given and cannot be purchased. It is simply earned, acquired by a relentless will to persevere and overcome.

Instead of viewing failure as a dead end, view failure as a stepping-stone on a path to success. Through failure, we learn, adapt, grow, and ultimately succeed. As explored throughout this book, failure, along with life's challenges, is an integral part of the human experience. Challenges, grief, and failure are all nondiscriminatory events that will touch us all at some point in our lives. Rather than fearing failure, accepting and understanding this fundamental concept positions us for success in any situation. Additionally, we must face the implications of our past and move forward with an optimistic approach. In doing so, we begin to utilize our past "failures" to build the future while highlighting our ability to take control of our lives.

In a speech delivered at the Sorbonne in Paris, France, on April 23rd, 1910, Theodore Roosevelt gave his historic "Man in the Arena" speech. The speech highlighted the duties and responsibilities of the state to its citizens as well as the citizens to the state. The famous "Man in the Arena" passage addresses the importance of taking action and striving towards worthy goals in lieu of being an idle critic with an unwillingness to take action or fail.

"It is not the critic who counts; not the man who points out how the strong man stumbles, or where the doer of deeds could have done them better. The credit belongs to the man who is actually in the arena, whose face is marred by dust and sweat and blood; who strives valiantly; who errs, who comes short again and again, because there is no effort without error and shortcoming; but who does actually strive to do the deeds; who knows great enthusiasms, the great devotions; who spends himself in a worthy cause; who at the best knows in the end the triumph of high achievement, and who at the worst, if he fails, at least fails while daring greatly, so that his place shall never be with those cold and timid souls who neither know victory nor defeat.... There is little use for the being whose tepid soul knows nothing of great and generous emotion, of the high pride, the stern belief, the lofty enthusiasm, of the men who quell the storm and ride the thunder" (Theodore Roosevelt, 1910).

In the midst of our challenges, have we accepted avoidance as a solution? Are we making life harder because we simply refuse to act? Again, what is success without failure? In life, there is no gain without loss. With a little imagination and the willingness to take the first step, we begin to unlock a world full of possibilities. Following the success of the light bulb, Thomas Edison highlighted the unforeseen opportunities gained from persevering through failure, stating, "We are striking it big in the electric light, better than my vivid imagination first conceived. Where this thing is going to stop, Lord only knows." Although the outcome may not be well-defined, it is clear that if we are willing, the future will always be better than the past.

"Failure is success in progress."
—Albert Einstein

Failing Forward
Workshop

Workshop:
Personal Development

In this section of the book, we will highlight previously discussed development approaches, provide practical insights, thought-provoking reflections, and actionable steps to move forward. At the end of each section, reflection questions are provided to encourage us to take our time, foster a deeper understanding of ourselves, and uncover the necessary actions for growth. The questions aim to guide introspection and personal growth across various aspects of life.

Internal Motivation

The journey begins within. To be an effective leader, we must first ignite the flame of internal motivation. This section explores the power of self-motivation and encourages us to understand our values, passions, and the driving forces that propel them forward. Those seeking self-help should start by understanding our intrinsic drivers and uncovering what truly inspires and excites us.

Developing our internal motivation is a multifaceted process that requires understanding our needs, fostering a sense of purpose, and cultivating intrinsic motivation. Motivating ourselves goes well beyond external rewards and taps into our personal values, aspirations, and beliefs. Here's a comprehensive analysis of strategies to drive internal motivation, enabling us to act, move forward, overcome, and ultimately succeed.

Align goals with internal motivations: Rather than pursuing external validations, focus on goals that resonate with personal values and contribute to a sense of fulfillment. This creates a sustainable source of internal motivation that extends well beyond external rewards. Foster a growth mindset by viewing challenges and setbacks as opportunities for learning and improvement. Embrace the belief that abilities can be developed through dedication and hard work.

Self-Reflection: Be encouraged to engage in self-reflection to identify your core values and long-term goals. Understanding what truly matters to you provides a foundation for sustaining your intrinsic motivation.

Impact and Contribution: Highlight the positive impacts you can have on others within your community.

Autonomy and Mastery: Provide opportunities for autonomy and skill development. Take ownership of your tasks and cultivate support. You have the ability, sense of control, and autonomy over your decisions. Realize you have the power to make decisions and take action. Internal motivation is more likely to thrive when we accept that we have the power to determine the outcome.

Personalized Approaches: When encouraging others, identify and respect individual differences. Tailor your approach to motivate others based on their preferences, strengths, and unique characteristics.

Celebrate Achievements: Acknowledge and celebrate both small and significant achievements. Celebrations serve as positive reinforcement, reinforcing the idea that effort leads to success. The key is to nurture a sense of purpose and passion that empowers you to find fulfillment and meaning in your pursuits.

Share Your Journey: Share your experiences with others. Inspiring others through your journey not only reinforces your own growth but also creates a positive impact on the community around you.

Acknowledge Inner Strength: Reflect on and acknowledge your inner strength. Recognizing your capacity to overcome adversity and navigate change reinforces your self-efficacy and motivation.

<u>Reflection Questions</u>

➤ Beyond external factors, what truly motivates you from within?

➤ Are you pursuing goals for genuine personal fulfillment, or are you driven by external expectations?

➤ How do you envision the legacy you want to leave for your family and community?

➤ Are your current goals aligned with your core values and long-term vision for a purposeful life?

➤ What is currently holding you back from being who you desire to be? List practical ways to remove these roadblocks.

Overcoming Adversity

Overcoming adversity and navigating through change are integral aspects of personal growth and resilience. Both involve facing challenges, uncertainties, and disruptions, but they also present opportunities for learning and transformation. Here is a comprehensive analysis of useful strategies to overcome adversity and navigate change successfully.

Life is a journey marked by peaks and valleys; embrace it with a challenger's mindset. This section addresses the inevitability of adversity and provides a roadmap to navigate through challenging times. Drawing inspiration from stories of resilience and triumph, we discuss strategies for overcoming obstacles, teaching us to view adversity not as a roadblock but as a steppingstone towards personal growth.

Resilience in the Face of Challenges: Overcoming adversity requires resilience. We can build resilience by reframing challenges as opportunities for growth. Embrace setbacks as part of the journey and focus on learning from and adapting to adversity.

Seeking Support: It's crucial to recognize the strength of seeking support. Whether from family, friends, church, or professional networks, having a support system can provide valuable perspectives, advice, and encouragement during challenging times. Isolating from those who can help often leads to misappropriation of valuable time and later becomes a self-destructive decline to the bottom. Instead, consider support as an asset within your toolbox that can be used for growth and success.

Mindfulness and Stress Management: Incorporate mindfulness and stress management practices to navigate adversity effectively. Techniques such as meditation, deep breathing, and positive visualization can enhance emotional well-being and help maintain focus during tough situations.

Acceptance of Reality: Acknowledge the reality of the adversity or change. Acceptance is the first step towards building resilience. Avoiding denial and facing the situation head-on fosters a resilient mindset.

Positive Reframing: Practice reframing negative thoughts into positive ones. Instead of viewing adversity as insurmountable, see it as an opportunity for growth and learning. This shift in perspective enhances resilience.

Focus on What You Can Control: Identify aspects of the situation that you can control and focus your energy on those. A sense of control helps reduce feelings of helplessness and empowers you to take constructive actions.

Adaptability and Flexibility
Embrace Change as a Constant: Accept that change is inevitable. Embracing change as a constant part of life fosters adaptability. The ability to adapt to new circumstances is crucial for overcoming adversity. View setbacks as opportunities for learning and growth. Use the Three A's (Accept, Assess, Adjust) to analyze what went wrong, identify lessons, and apply them to future situations.

Develop Problem-Solving Skills: Cultivate problem-solving skills to address challenges systematically. Break down complex issues into manageable tasks and approach them one step at a time. This approach enhances your ability to navigate change effectively.

Set Realistic Goals

Define Clear Objectives: Set realistic and achievable goals to guide your actions. Being able to achieve realistic milestones can provides us with a sense of progress and accomplishment, fueling ongoing motivation.

Adjust Goals as Needed: Be flexible with your goals and adjust them based on evolving circumstances. The ability to adapt one's goals demonstrates resilience and a willingness to navigate change effectively.

Growth with Adversity

Embrace a Learning Mindset: Approach adversity and change with a learning mindset. View challenges as opportunities to acquire new skills, gain insights, and grow personally and professionally.

Seek Feedback: Solicit feedback from others to gain different perspectives and identify areas for improvement. Constructive feedback contributes to your learning journey and enhances your ability to adapt.

Maintain a Positive Outlook

Practice Gratitude: Cultivate a practice of gratitude. Focus on aspects of your life that bring joy and fulfillment, even during challenging times. Gratitude creates a shift in our mindset providing us with a positive outlook on what we have and what can be achieved.

Optimism and Hope: Nurture optimism and hope. Believing in your ability to overcome challenges. Reflect on past accomplishments and continue to push yourself one step at a time.

Time Management and Prioritization

Effective Time Management: Develop effective time management skills to prioritize tasks and allocate resources efficiently. Organizing your time allows for a more structured and focused approach to overcoming challenges.

Set Priorities: Clearly define priorities to allocate energy to the most critical aspects of the situation. Setting priorities helps prevent feeling overwhelmed and ensures a strategic approach to change and adversity.

Create Action Plans: Develop action plans with clear steps and timelines. Having a roadmap provides a sense of direction and control, facilitating effective navigation through adversity and change.

Inspire a Vision of Success

Visualization: Creating a mental image of achieving goals can serve as a powerful motivator, helping us to stay focused on our aspirations, regardless of their inherent challenges.

Storytelling and Role Models: Gather stories and reflect on life experiences of past success or individuals who have overcome challenges. Positive learning experiences, role models, and success stories can inspire and serve as benchmarks for what is achievable.

Developing resilience, fostering adaptability, and maintaining a positive outlook contribute to the ability to not only overcome challenges but also thrive in the face of uncertainty and change. By embracing personal growth and continuous learning, we can build the inner strength needed to successfully navigate life's inevitable ups and downs.

Reflection Questions

➢ Reflect on a challenging experience—what did you learn from it, and how did it shape who you are today?

➢ How do you approach adversity, and what strategies can you employ to navigate difficult situations more effectively?

➢ What role does attitude and/or fear play in how you perceive and respond to challenges?

➢ How can you reframe setbacks as opportunities for growth and learning?

➢ What strengths and resources do you currently possess that can help you overcome adversity? What weaknesses do you need to improve?

Taking Risks and Failing Forward

Taking risks is an integral part of personal and professional growth. We must learn to embrace calculated risks and view failure as a valuable teacher, not only for ourselves but for our families as well. This section explores the concept of failing forward, encouraging us to see setbacks as opportunities for learning and refinement. From the perspective of being a father, fathers can cultivate an environment with a mindset that values risk-taking and resilience, instilling a sense of courage and adaptability in their children.

Calculating Risks and Rewards: Learning to take risks involves making a calculated assessment of potential rewards. Evaluating risks in both personal and professional contexts and weighing the potential benefits against the drawbacks is a great way to drive action. This strategic approach minimizes reckless behavior and formulates a game plan to achieve a successful outcome.

Embracing a "Fail Forward" Mentality: The concept of "failing forward" identifies and accepts that we all fail. The concept highlights the progress of reaching forward instead of allowing life to push us backwards. Rather than fearing failure, "failing forward" embraces challenges as a natural part of the journey towards success. This approach extracts lessons learned from failures and uses them to improve in future endeavors.

Encouraging a Growth Mindset in Children: Instill a growth mindset in children by fostering a positive attitude towards challenges. Teach them that taking risks and facing failures are integral to learning and growth.

Encourage curiosity, resilience, and a willingness to explore new opportunities.

Innovation and Creativity

Fostering Innovation: Failure is often a precursor to innovation. Creative breakthroughs and novel ideas frequently emerge from the lessons learned through unsuccessful attempts. Embracing failure as part of the creative process encourages experimentation and exploration.

Personal Growth and Development

Learning About Yourself: Failure provides valuable insights into one's strengths, weaknesses, and areas for improvement. The process of reflection after failure allows individuals to gain a deeper understanding of themselves and their capabilities.

Overcoming Limiting Beliefs: Failure challenges limiting beliefs and self-imposed barriers. When individuals confront and overcome failures, they often realize that perceived limitations are not insurmountable, leading to increased self-confidence and personal growth.

Career and Professional Development

Entrepreneurial Mindset: Entrepreneurs often view failure as an integral part of the entrepreneurial journey. Embracing failure, learning from it, and adapting business strategies accordingly are essential components of an entrepreneurial mindset.

Leadership and Decision-Making: Effective leaders recognize the value of learning from failure.

Leaders who openly acknowledge and address failures foster a culture of continuous improvement, encouraging their teams to take calculated risks and innovate.

Encouraging a Supportive Environment: Creating a supportive environment where individuals feel comfortable sharing their failures without fear of judgment is essential. Create an environment that celebrates learning from failures while fostering collaboration and continuous improvement.

Goal Setting and Planning: When failures occur, revisiting goals and adjusting plans based on lessons learned contributes to a more informed and resilient approach.

Transparency and Communication: Transparent communication about failures is essential in organizational settings. Leaders who openly communicate about failures, share insights, and outline corrective actions contribute to a culture of trust and openness.

Learning from Ethical Missteps: In cases where failures involve ethical lapses, learning from those missteps is paramount. Individuals must implement corrective measures, ensure accountability, and integrate ethical considerations into future decision-making.

By changing perspectives on failure, embracing a growth mindset, and adopting strategies for reflection and adaptation, individuals and organizations can harness the positive potential of failure as a stepping-stone towards success. The ability to learn from failures is not only a measure of individual and collective resilience but also a driving force behind continuous improvement, innovation, and societal progress.

<u>**Reflection Questions**</u>

➢ Have you embraced opportunities that required stepping out of your comfort zone? If not, what's holding you back?

➢ How do you view failure, and how can you use it as a steppingstone towards success?

➢ What was the biggest risk you've taken in your life? How did it shape your personal growth?

➢ Recall a failed experience that ultimately led to a positive outcome or learning opportunity.

➢ Looking back at your life, what advice would you give your younger self about embracing failure and taking risks?

Continuous Self-Reflection and Learning

Schedule Self-Reflection: Set aside time for routine self-reflection. Continue to assess personal values, goals, and achievements. Periodically revisit and adjust priorities to align with evolving aspirations. This self-awareness contributes to intentional decision-making and purposeful living.

Learning and Development: The pursuit of knowledge and skills for personal growth can be a powerful source that fuels internal motivation to act. Cultivate curiosity and a willingness to explore new possibilities.

Adaptability: Emphasize the importance of adaptability. Those who are open to change and see it as an opportunity for growth are more likely to be internally motivated in the face of evolving circumstances. If responsibilities or goals need adjustment, be willing to make changes. Adaptability enhances our ability to navigate life's complexities with resilience.

Reflection Questions

➢ What new skills or knowledge can you acquire to enhance your personal and professional growth?

➢ Are you open to learning from others and embracing new perspectives?

➢ What are you grateful for? And how can you express this gratitude to those who matter most?

➢ How can a mindset of gratitude positively impact my overall well-being?

➢ How do you distinguish between calculated risks and reckless decisions in your own life?

Cultivating Emotional Intelligence

Understanding and Expressing Emotions: Emotional intelligence is essential for effective self-help and leadership. We can cultivate emotional intelligence by understanding and expressing our emotions in a constructive way. Leading the way, we can encourage open communication within our own families as we foster stronger emotional behaviors.

Empathy in Relationships: Understanding the emotions of family members, colleagues, and community members builds strong connections. Empathy and conflict resolution fosters a supportive environment and contributes to effective leadership and positive interactions.

Effective Communication: Learn to communicate your emotions and needs effectively. Clear communication fosters understanding and helps build a support system.

Reflection Questions

➢ How do you communicate with your family members, and how can you strengthen these connections?

➢ Are you actively listening to others? How can you improve your communication skills?

➢ In what ways do you think fear of failure holds people back from taking risks and pursuing their goals?

➢ How do you typically respond to criticism or feedback, and what does this say about your emotional resilience?

➢ Do you recognize when your emotions are influencing your thoughts and behaviors? How can you regulate them in these moments?

Holistic Approach to Well-Being

Physical Well-Being: Prioritize physical health through regular exercise, a balanced diet, and sufficient sleep. Physical well-being positively impacts mental and emotional resilience.

Mindfulness and Stress Reduction: Practice mindfulness and stress reduction techniques. Techniques such as meditation, deep breathing, running, or any form of exercise can help manage stress and enhance your ability to cope with adversity.

Work-Life Integration: Achieve a manageable work-life integration. Balancing professional and personal responsibilities allows for sustained well-being and contributes to a positive family environment. Set boundaries, manage time effectively, and make time for valuable time with family members. Nurture positive connections that will contribute to a sense of belonging and a support system. Having strong social bonds is essential for overall well-being and resilience during challenging times.

Cultivate Intrinsic Passion

Identify Passions: Connecting tasks to your intrinsic passions can significantly boost morale and motivation, as these activities reinforce both joy and fulfillment. While fulfilling duties to family, career, and community, prioritize self-care and well-being. Personal fulfillment enhances our ability to positively impact others in various roles.

Encourage Pursuit of Interests: Continue to pursue personal interests, outside of immediate responsibilities. New challenges often shed light on undiscovered interests. With new interest, we begin to broaden our understanding of our capabilities, gaining confidence with pursuit.

Healthy Coping Mechanisms: Foster healthy coping mechanisms, such as engaging in hobbies, spending time in nature, or connecting with loved ones. These activities provide outlets for stress and contribute to overall well-being.

d

<u>**Reflection Questions**</u>

➢ Do you prioritize your mental and emotional well-being?

➢ What activities bring you joy and fulfillment? Are you making time for them?

➢ How well are you balancing your personal and professional life? What adjustments can you make?

➢ Do you allocate time for self-care and personal growth amid your responsibilities?

➢ Do you set and maintain healthy boundaries in different aspects of life?

Responsibility

Responsibility is the cornerstone of being a husband and a father. This section explores the profound connection between assuming responsibilities and discovering your true purpose. We are challenged to reflect on the impact of our actions, decisions, and commitments, understanding the effects we have on our families and communities. Through a sense of purpose rooted in responsibility, we are able to find fulfillment and develop a deeper connection to our role as leaders and mentors.

Aligning Responsibilities with Values: Discovering true purpose involves aligning responsibilities with personal values. We can reflect on our roles and responsibilities, ensuring that they resonate with our core beliefs and contribute to a meaningful life.

Sense of Contribution and Impact

Making a Difference: Discovering purpose through increased responsibility often involves a desire to make a meaningful difference. We may find fulfillment in knowing that our actions contribute to the overall well-being of others.

Legacy and Long-Term Impact: As responsibilities grow, individuals may start contemplating their legacy and long-term impact. A sense of purpose extends beyond immediate tasks when we consider the lasting influence and positive change we can leave for future generations.

Meaning in Responsibility: Taking on responsibility is a fundamental aspect of living a meaningful life. Responsibility is a tool for confronting chaos in our own lives. Responsibility also provides a sense of order within our own existence. Engaging with challenges and taking on meaningful tasks can contribute to our personal growth, resilience, and deeper discovery of purpose.

Self-Determination Theory: Self-Determination Theory states that individuals are motivated by the need for autonomy, competence, and relatedness. Increased responsibility can fulfill our psychological needs by fostering intrinsic motivation and a sense of purpose.

Mastery and Competence: Taking on greater responsibilities provides opportunities for mastery and competence. Achieving success in tasks that challenge and stretch our abilities can enhance our self-esteem.

Connection to Intrinsic Motivation

Intrinsic vs. Extrinsic Motivation: In the realm of responsibility, intrinsic motivation plays a vital role. While external rewards may exist, the intrinsic satisfaction derived from meaningful tasks and responsibilities becomes the driving force in discovering and sustaining purpose.

<u>Reflection Questions</u>

➢ What responsibilities do you currently hold, and how do they contribute to your sense of purpose?

➢ In what ways can you align your responsibilities with your deeper values and aspirations?

➢ Have you ever experienced a shift in perspective or purpose as a result of fulfilling a particular responsibility or obligation?

➢ In what ways can taking ownership of your responsibilities lead to personal growth and self-discovery?

➢ How do your responsibilities shape your values and priorities?

Motivational Quotes

&

Bible Verses

❖ "Life can only be understood backwards; but it must be lived forwards."—Søren Kierkegaard

❖ "A successful person begins with two beliefs: the future can be better than the present, and I have the power to make it so."—David Brooks

❖ "The only way to do great work is to love what you do."—Steve Jobs

❖ "Believe you can and you're halfway there." —Theodore Roosevelt

❖ "Success is not final, failure is not fatal: It is the courage to continue that counts."—Winston Churchill

❖ "The only limit to our realization of tomorrow will be our doubts of today."—Franklin D. Roosevelt

❖ "The future belongs to those who believe in the beauty of their dreams."—Eleanor Roosevelt

❖ "The only person you are destined to become is the person you decide to be."—Ralph Waldo Emerson

❖ "The function of prayer is not to influence God, but rather to change the nature of the one who prays." —Søren Kierkegaard

❖ "Success is not the key to happiness. Happiness is the key to success. If you love what you are doing, you will be successful."—Albert Schweitzer

❖ "To dare is to lose one's footing momentarily. To not dare is to lose oneself."—Søren Kierkegaard

❖ "Your limitation—it's only your imagination." —Unknown

❖ "Don't wait. The time will never be just right." —Napoleon Hill

❖ "The only way to achieve the impossible is to believe it is possible."—Charles Kingsleigh (*Alice in Wonderland*)

❖ "Opportunities don't happen. You create them." —Chris Grosser

❖ "Don't watch the clock; do what it does. Keep going."—Sam Levenson

❖ "You are never too old to set another goal or to dream a new dream."—C. S. Lewis

❖ "Success is walking from failure to failure with no loss of enthusiasm."—Winston Churchill

❖ "The harder you work for something, the greater you'll feel when you achieve it."—Unknown

❖ "The secret of getting ahead is getting started."
—Mark Twain

❖ "The only place where success comes before work is
in the dictionary."—Vidal Sassoon

❖ "It's not whether you get knocked down, it's whether
you get up."—Vince Lombardi

❖ "Life is not a problem to be solved, but a reality to be
experienced."—Søren Kierkegaard

❖ "The only limit to our realization of tomorrow will be
our doubts of today."—Franklin D. Roosevelt

❖ "Dream big and dare to fail."—Norman Vaughan

❖ "You don't have to be great to start, but you have to
start to be great."—Zig Ziglar

❖ "Face the facts of being what you are, for that is what
changes what you are."—Søren Kierkegaard

❖ "Success is not how high you have climbed, but how
you make a positive difference to the world."
—Roy T. Bennett

❖ "Anxiety is the dizziness of freedom."—Søren
Kierkegaard

❖ "The way to get started is to quit talking and begin
doing."—Walt Disney

❖ "The only thing standing between you and your goal is the story you keep telling yourself as to why you can't achieve it."—Jordan Belfort

❖ "I can do all things through Christ who strengthens me."—Philippians 4:13

❖ "Trust in the Lord with all your heart and lean not on your own understanding."—Proverbs 3:5

❖ "For I know the plans I have for you, declares the Lord, plans to prosper you and not to harm you, plans to give you hope and a future."—Jeremiah 29:11

❖ "Be strong and courageous. Do not be afraid; do not be discouraged, for the Lord your God will be with you wherever you go."—Joshua 1:9

❖ "But those who hope in the Lord will renew their strength. They will soar on wings like eagles; they will run and not grow weary, they will walk and not be faint."—Isaiah 40:31

❖ "For God gave us a spirit not of fear but of power and love and self-control."—2 Timothy 1:7

❖ "And we know that in all things God works for the good of those who love him, who have been called according to his purpose."—Romans 8:28

❖ "Let us not become weary in doing good, for at the proper time we will reap a harvest if we do not give up."—Galatians 6:9

❖ "Commit to the Lord whatever you do, and he will establish your plans."—Proverbs 16:3

❖ "The Lord is my strength and my shield; my heart trusts in him, and he helps me. My heart leaps for joy, and with my song I praise him."—Psalm 28:7

References

Dolcos, S., Hu, Y., Iordan, A. D., Moore, M., & Dolcos, F. (2016). Optimism and the brain: trait optimism mediates the protective role of the orbitofrontal cortex gray matter volume against anxiety. *Social Cognitive and Affective Neuroscience, 11*(2), 263–271. doi:10.1093/scan/nsv106

Peterson, J. B. (1999). *Maps of meaning: The architecture of belief.* Routledge. https://doi.org/10.4324/9780203902851

US Burden of Disease Collaborators. (2013). The state of US health, 1990–2010: Burden of diseases, injuries, and risk factors. *JAMA: The Journal of the American Medical Association, 310*(6), 591–608. doi:10.1001/jama.2013.13805

Resources

Here are organizations that provide information and resources for fathers, highlighting the important roles they play in the lives of their children. If you are aware of any others, please contact Child Welfare Information Gateway at OrganizationUpdates@childwelfare.gov.

All Pro Dad Chapters

5509 W. Gray Street
Suite #100
Tampa, FL 33609
Phone: (813) 222-8300
Email: allprodadsday@familyfirst.net
All Pro Dad, the fatherhood program of Family First, is a national nonprofit educational and charitable organization committed to serving fathers around the world with a focus on providing guidance and practical tips for raising children.
nadid: 30207

Center for Family Policy and Practice

23 North Pinckney Street
Suite 304
Madison, WI 53703
Phone: (608) 257-3148
The Center for Family Policy and Practice is a nationally focused public policy organization conducting policy research, technical assistance, training, litigation, and public education in order to focus attention on the barriers faced by never-married, low-income fathers and their families. Current primary projects include domestic

violence and fatherhood and child welfare and
fatherhood policy.
nadid: 12584

Child Welfare Information Gateway

Children's Bureau/ACYF
330 C Street, S.W.
Washington, DC 20201
Toll-Free: (800) 394-3366
Email: info@childwelfare.gov
Child Welfare Information Gateway connects
professionals and the general public to information and
resources targeted to the safety, permanency, and well-
being of children and families. A service of the
Children's Bureau, Administration for Children and
Families, U.S. Department of Health and Human
Services, Child Welfare Information Gateway provides
access to programs, research, laws and policies, training
resources, statistics, and much more.
nadid: 17904

FatherhoodFirst.org

Youth & Family Services
PO Box 2813
Rapid City, SD 57709-2813
Phone: (605) 342-4233
The mission of FatherhoodFirst.org is to help fathers
develop positive relationships with their children and to
help them understand the importance of their presence in
the lives of their children. At Fatherhood First, fathers are
offered father/child activities (both in group and
individual settings), one-on-one case management
classes for new and expectant fathers, and male

involvement meetings to families within our community. FatherhoodFirst.org makes these same resources and activities available to Head Start programs nationwide. The FatherhoodFirst.org project was made possible through funding from the U.S. Department of Health and Human Services Administration for Children and Families Office of Head Start.
nadid: 18711

Fatherville.com
2540 W Glade Creek Street
Meridian, ID 83646
Phone: (208) 887-9086
Fatherville.com is an online resource ONLY that supports, encourages, and challenges fathers in every stage of fatherhood. Fatherville.com's mission and goal are to encourage men to become better fathers through the exchange of ideas. This exchange can take place in a number of ways: via the online forum, written essays, and contributed articles from other fathers.
nadid: 18710

National Center for Fathering (NCF)
PO Box 2865
Olathe, KS 66063
Phone: (913) 222-9494
Toll-Free: (800) 593-3237
Email: admin@fathers.com
The mission of the National Center for Fathering (NCF) is to improve the well-being of children by inspiring and equipping men to be more effectively involved in their lives. The Center conducts research on fathers and

fathering, and it develops practical resources to prepare dads for nearly every fathering situation.
nadid: 25532

National Fatherhood Initiative
12410 Milestone Center Drive
Suite 600
Germantown, MD 20876
Phone: (301) 948-0599
Email: info@fatherhood.org
The National Fatherhood Initiative works to improve the well-being of children by increasing the proportion of children growing up with involved, responsible, and committed fathers.
nadid: 11197

National Parents Organization
P.O. Box 590548
Newton, MA 02459
Phone: (617) 431-8019
The National Parents Organization focuses on advocacy and research leading to systemic reform of the family courts.
nadid: 30364

National Responsible Fatherhood Clearinghouse (NRFC)
2394 Mt. Vernon Road
Suite 210
Dunwoody, GA 30338
Phone: (703) 225-2320
Toll-Free: (877) 432-3411
Email: Help@FatherhoodGov.Info

The National Responsible Fatherhood Clearinghouse (NRFC) supports the Administration for Children and Families' Office of Family Assistance's (OFA) efforts to assist States and communities to promote and support Responsible Fatherhood and Healthy Marriage.

Primarily a tool for professionals operating Responsible Fatherhood programs, the NRFC provides access to print and electronic publications, timely information on fatherhood issues, and targeted resources that support OFA-funded Responsible Fatherhood and Healthy Marriage recipients. The NRFC website also provides essential information for other audiences interested in fatherhood issues.
nadid: 19982

Native American Fatherhood & Family Association (NAFFA)
525 West Southern Avenue
Suite 100
Mesa, AZ 85210
Phone: (480) 833-5007
Email: info@aznaffa.org
The mission of the Native American Fatherhood & Families Association (NAFFA) is to strengthen Native American families by encouraging fathers to become more actively involved in the lives of their children, families, and communities. NAFFA also strives to strengthen the father's role by fostering communication, education, and collaboration among professional service providers.
nadid: 19692

U.S. Department of Health and Human Services (HHS), Administration for Children and Families (ACF)

330 C Street S.W.

Washington, DC 20201

Phone: (202) 619-0257

Toll-Free: (877) 696-6675

HHS is the government agency responsible for protecting the health of Americans. While the website (http://www.hhs.gov) covers a much broader range of health issues, the Administration for Children and Families (ACF) is devoted to families and children and specific populations such as minorities, fathers, and the disabled.

nadid: 11115

Washington State Fathers Network

Kindering Center

19801 North Creek Parkway

Bothell, WA 98011

Phone: (425) 653-4286

The Fathers Network provides current information and resources to assist all families and care providers involved in the lives of children with special needs.

nadid: 1258

About the Author

Brian Lockridge, Founder of Girl Dad USA, is a dedicated husband, proud father of two daughters, and a passionate advocate for personal and professional growth. A former running back for the University of Colorado with success both on and off the field, he was honored with the prestigious Allstate AFCA Good Works Team® award for his commitment to community service and leadership.

After his time on the football field, Brian transitioned seamlessly into the corporate world, where he leveraged his leadership skills and competitive spirit to excel in various leadership roles within Fortune 500 companies. With a knack for team building and development, Brian has led and mentored teams to achieve outstanding results, earning recognition for his innovative strategies and collaborative approach.

Outside of his professional endeavors, Brian is deeply committed to giving back and making a positive impact in the lives of others. Whether coaching youth sports teams, volunteering at local charities, or mentoring young athletes, Brian is dedicated to empowering others to reach their full potential and make a difference in the world.

Brian brings a unique blend of athleticism, leadership, and service to his work, inspiring readers to overcome obstacles, embrace challenges, and strive for excellence in all areas of life. With his engaging storytelling and practical insights, Brian aims to motivate and empower individuals to unleash their inner potential and achieve their goals.

Girl Dad USA

At Girl Dad USA, our mission is to empower fathers and father figures to lead, encourage, and cultivate a nurturing and positive environment for the long-term development of their daughters. We believe that a father's role is not just that of a protector, but a mentor, a guide, and a steadfast source of love and support.

Our Commitment:

- ❖ Lead with Love
- ❖ Encourage Exploration
- ❖ Foster Self-Confidence
- ❖ Promote Education
- ❖ Nurture Emotional Intelligence
- ❖ Instill Values
- ❖ Celebrate Individuality
- ❖ Support Independence
- ❖ Create Lasting Memories
- ❖ Prepare for the Future

Through our unwavering commitment to these principles, Girl Dad USA aspires to empower fathers and father figures to be the guiding lights in their daughters' lives, ensuring their long-term development, happiness, and success. Together, we aim to build a brighter and more equitable future for the girls who will shape tomorrow's world.

For More Information:
Visit: www.GirlDadUSA.com

www.ingramcontent.com/pod-product-compliance
Lightning Source LLC
Chambersburg PA
CBHW051223120626
46547CB00013B/1486